ACTS

BOOKS OF FAITH SERIES
Learner Session Guide

Ray Pickett

AUGSBURG FORTRESS

Minneapolis

ACTS
Learner Session Guide

Books of Faith Series
Book of Faith Adult Bible Studies

Book of Faith is an initiative of the
Evangelical Lutheran Church in America
God's work. Our hands.

For more information about the Book of Faith initiative, go to www.bookoffaith.org.

References to ELW are from *Evangelical Lutheran Worship* (Augsburg Fortress, 2006).

Web site addresses are provided in this resource for your use. These listings do not represent an endorsement of the sites by Augsburg Fortress, nor do we vouch for their content for the life of this resource.

ISBN: 978-1-4514-0274-2
Writer: Ray Pickett
Cover and interior design: Spunk Design Machine, spkdm.com
Typesetting: PerfecType, Nashville, TN

The paper used in this publication meets the minimum requirements of American National Standard for Information Sciences—Permanence of Paper for Printed Library Materials, ANSI Z329.48-1984.

Manufactured in the U.S.A.
18 17 16 15 14 13 12 1 2 3 4 5 6 7 8 9 10

CONTENTS

Acts 2:1-47

Learner Session Guide

Focus Statement
The Spirit that anointed Jesus to proclaim good news to the poor and release to the captives is poured out on an international group of Jews in Jerusalem. The gift to speak in other languages signals the fulfillment of God's promise to restore Israel and gather the nations into the covenant community of God's people.

Key Verse
"This Jesus God raised up, and of that all of us are witnesses. Being therefore exalted at the right hand of God, and having received from the Father the promise of the Holy Spirit, he has poured out this that you both see and hear." Acts 2:32-33

The Spirit Creates Community

Focus Image

Pentecost, All rights reserved. Vie de Jésus MAFA, 24 rue du Maréchal Joffre, F-78000 VERSAILLES, France, www.jesusmafa.com

Gather

Check-in

Take this time to connect or reconnect with the others in your group and give a special welcome to newcomers. Today we begin our study of Acts with the story of Pentecost and the founding of the early church. Thousands of Jewish pilgrims from nations far and near would have been gathered in Jerusalem for the feast of Pentecost. When the disciples are filled with the Holy Spirit, people are able to understand them in their own languages.

Pray

Almighty and ever-living God, you fulfilled the promise of Easter by sending the gift of your Holy Spirit. Look upon your people gathered in prayer, open to receive the Spirit's flame. May it come to rest in our hearts and heal the divisions of word and tongue, that with one voice and one song we may praise your name in joy and thanksgiving; through Jesus Christ, our Savior and Lord, who lives and reigns with you and the Holy Spirit, one God, now and forever. Amen.
(Prayer of the Day for Vigil of Pentecost, ELW p. 36)

Focus Activity

The Focus Image is a depiction of the outpouring of the Spirit at Pentecost. The people in this picture respond to the Spirit's

Notes

activity in their midst in a variety of ways. Briefly describe these responses. Which person's face or response best describes your own experience of the Spirit?

Open Scripture

Read Acts 2:1-47.

- As you listen to the passage, what words or phrases speak to you?

- How is the activity of the Spirit described in this text?

- What questions does this raise for you?

Join the Conversation

Literary Context

1. The Acts of the Apostles is the second volume of a two-volume work that includes the Gospel of Luke. Acts tells the story of how the ministry of Jesus continues and is extended through the community of followers after his resurrection and ascension. The major themes in Luke are developed in Acts through the stories of faithful followers of Jesus who have been empowered by the Spirit to bear witness to his resurrection, which sets in motion the restoration of Israel and the nations.

- Acts opens with a scene of the risen Jesus reminding his disciples that "John baptized with water, but you will be baptized with the Holy Spirit not many days from now" (Acts 1:5). Read Acts 1:6-8. What is the role and purpose of the Spirit that is poured out on Jesus' followers on Pentecost?

2. The theme of Israel's restoration frames Luke's story of Jesus, and the hope that the risen Jesus would now "restore the kingdom to Israel" is repeated in the disciples' question in Acts 1:6.

• Reread Acts 2:1-47 and identify some signs of restoration in the relationships between the Jews and God and among one another.

 Notes

3. Bearing witness to the risen Jesus is another important theme and activity in Acts. Peter says, "This Jesus God raised up, and of that all of us are *witnesses*" (2:32). Those who are filled with the Holy Spirit at Pentecost speak in other languages about "God's deeds of power" (2:11).

• What does it mean to bear witness to Jesus' resurrection today? Brainstorm a list of practical ways you might bear witness to the risen Jesus in your congregation and in your life.

4. Repentance is another major theme in the Gospel of Luke and in Acts. The call to repentance is a call to consider what changes we need to make to live in accordance with God's life-giving purposes.

• Read Luke 3:7-14 and Acts 2:37-42. Compare and contrast John's baptism of repentance in Luke with Peter's call for repentance in Acts.

• What would repentance look like for us? How would it affect our habits of thought and action?

• What specific attitudes and practices might we adopt if we were to take seriously Peter's admonition to "save yourselves from this corrupt generation" (Acts 2:40)?

Historical Context

1. Acts has much in common with ancient historical writings. These ancient writings were not simply reports of what had happened. Acts not only tells about Jesus' ministry, death, and resurrection; it also shows that these events happened according to God's purposes. So in speaking of the historical event of Jesus' crucifixion, Peter says: "This man, handed over to you *according to the definite plan and foreknowledge of God*, you crucified and killed by the hands of those outside the law" (Acts 2:23).

• From a strictly historical perspective, all those listening to Peter's Pentecost sermon could not have been responsible for Jesus' execution. What is the significance of implicating everyone in the audience? What does that mean for us?

2. Acts 2:41-47 is one of the earliest descriptions of the pattern of life followed by believers in Jerusalem. Followers of the risen Jesus who were baptized "devoted themselves to the apostles' teaching and fellowship, to the breaking of bread and the prayers" and "had all things in common." The word "fellowship" in Greek is *koinonia*. It was used frequently in Greco-Roman society to depict a profound sharing among friends who had all things in common.

Notes

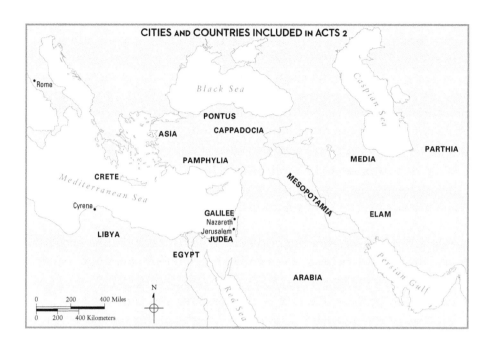

CITIES AND COUNTRIES INCLUDED IN ACTS 2

- Reflect on ways your congregation reflects the pattern of life together in Christ described in Acts 2:41-47. Also think about some new ways your congregation might embody this countercultural pattern of life.

Lutheran Context

1. A guiding principle of Lutheran biblical interpretation is *Scripture interprets Scripture*. This conviction is evident throughout Acts, which uses passages from the Jewish Scriptures (our Old Testament) to illuminate what is happening in the narrative. When people are filled with the Spirit and speak in other languages, Peter explains this in his Pentecost sermon by interpreting a passage from the prophet Joel.

- Read Acts 2:14-18 and Joel 2:28-29. What is the role of the Spirit in our attempts to interpret Scripture? How would you envision a fulfillment of such an outpouring of the Spirit in a Lutheran congregation today?

- Not just some but all people can be filled with the Spirit and endowed with gifts for witness and service. In line with this, Martin Luther emphasized that the vocation or calling of all the baptized is to serve and witness to Christ. How would we approach ministry and mission differently if we acted on the conviction that the Spirit works through people who hold different religious and political views and come from very different social and ethnic backgrounds?

2. Another important principle for Lutherans in interpreting the Bible is the relationship between *law* and *gospel*. Pentecost was originally a harvest festival, but it came to be associated with the giving of the law to Moses and the people. The Torah, or law, served as the basis for Jewish identity and moral order and therefore provided a sense of security and stability. However, the Spirit is depicted as divine energy that creates, inspires, restores, and empowers. It is unpredictable and uncontrollable and typically disrupts the status quo.

• Recall a time when you experienced the unsettling activity of the Spirit in your life. How did you respond?

Devotional Context

1. All who have been baptized into Christ have received the Spirit, but that is often regarded as a very personal and even private reality. The Pentecost story depicts the Spirit acting in very public ways.

• What does the session Scripture text have to say about the work of the Spirit in the world, the nation, the community, and your congregation?

• Reflect on what this text may be saying to you about new possibilities for living in the Spirit.

2. Historically, believers have used a variety of spiritual or faith practices, such as praying, worshiping, reading and studying the Bible, witnessing, serving, and giving in their efforts to live according to the Spirit. In Acts 2:1-47 being filled with the Spirit and a communal pattern of life are inextricably connected.

• What are some faith practices that would nurture your congregation's life together in the Spirit and empower you for witness and service?

Wrap-up

Be ready to look back over the work your group has done in this session.

Pray

Perplexing, Pentecostal God,
you infuse us with your Spirit,
urging us to vision and dream.
May the gift of your presence
find voice in our lives,
that our babbling may be transformed into discernment
and the flickering of many tongues
light an unquenchable fire of compassion and justice. Amen.
(*Revised Common Lectionary Prayers*, Augsburg Fortress, 2002)

 Notes

Notes

Extending the Conversation

Homework

1. Read the next session's Bible text: Acts 4:1-37.

2. Have a conversation with a member of your group or another person you know. Talk about how you see the Spirit at work in that person's life.

3. The call to repentance is not so much about regret or remorse as it is an invitation to reorient our habits of thought and action so that we can live in harmony with the Spirit. To repent is to contemplate what needs to change for us to live in the power of the Spirit. Make a list of some specific attitudes, perceptions, or behaviors you would like to change to bear witness to the risen Jesus in your life.

Enrichment

1. If you wish to read through the entire book of Acts during this unit, read the following sections this week:

Day 1: Acts 1:1-14
Day 2: Acts 1:15-26
Day 3: Acts 2:1-36
Day 4: Acts 2:37-47
Day 5: Acts 3:1-26
Day 6: Acts 4:1-22
Day 7: Acts 4:23-37

2. Throughout the Gospel of Luke and Acts, the Spirit works through Jesus and his followers to overcome boundaries and barriers for the sake of restoring people to community. In the Pentecost story the Spirit even overcomes the communication barrier of different languages. As you go about your week, pay close attention to the barriers that obstruct communication and community. Note instances where you see the Spirit at work in transcending obstacles to reconnect people to God and to one another.

3. The story of Pentecost is a story of people being filled and empowered by the Spirit to bear witness to the risen Jesus. As you go through the week, make note of the various ways power is expressed, especially in interpersonal relations. How is living in the power of the Spirit different from other kinds of personal, social, or political power? Be prepared to share some of your observations with the group at the next session.

4. Watch this dramatic and visual performance of the Pentecost story in Acts 2: http://www.youtube.com/watch?v=nOm1DMZJITs.

How does this performance of the text impact the way you read and understand it?

For Further Reading

Introduction to Acts and notes on Acts 2:1-47 in *Lutheran Study Bible* (Augsburg Fortress, 2009), *The HarperCollins Study Bible* (HarperOne, 2006), or *The New Oxford Annotated Bible* (Oxford University Press, 2010).

The Acts of the Apostles, by Luke Timothy Johnson. Collegeville, MN: Liturgical Press, 1992, pp. 41-63.

To Every Nation under Heaven: The Acts of the Apostles, by Howard Clark Kee. Harrisburg, PA: Trinity Press International, 1997, pp. 43-55.

Notes

Acts 4:1-37

Learner Session Guide

Focus Statement

The disciples are empowered to speak boldly about the resurrection of Jesus, bringing them into conflict with authorities. The people of the resurrection devote themselves to a pattern of life together, characterized by prayer and the sharing of possessions.

Key Verse

Now when they saw the boldness of Peter and John and realized that they were uneducated and ordinary men, they were amazed and recognized them as companions of Jesus.
Acts 4:13

The Empowering Spirit

 Focus Image

Chinese man stands alone to block a line of tanks heading east on Beijing's Cangan Blvd. in Tiananmen Square on June 5, 1989. AP Photo/Jeff Widener

Gather

Check-in

Take this time to connect or reconnect with the others in your group and give a special welcome to newcomers. Our study of Acts continues the story of the growth of the Jesus movement as those who were filled with the Spirit are arrested by the authorities and boldly bear witness to the Creator's power.

Pray

Almighty God, we praise you for your servants, through whom you have called the church to its tasks and renewed its life. Raise up in our own day teachers and prophets inspired by your Spirit, whose voices will give strength to your church and proclaim the reality of your reign, through Jesus Christ, our Savior and Lord, who lives and reigns with you and the Holy Spirit, one God, now and forever.
(adapted from Prayer for Renewers of the Church, ELW p. 60)

Focus Activity

The iconic and evocative image of the anonymous "tank man" in Beijing's Tiananmen Square in 1989 dramatically depicts two very different kinds of power or authority. While the tanks graphically represent the authority to overpower and suppress through control and subjugation, the man represents a very different kind of authority. How would you describe his power or authority? What is the source of his authority, and to what is he bearing this bold witness?

Open Scripture

Read Acts 4:1-37.

- As you listen to the passage with your heart, what words or phrases speak to you?

- What surprises you?

- What do you want to know more about?

Join the Conversation

Literary Context

1. The book of Acts opens with the risen Jesus telling the disciples they will be baptized with the Holy Spirit and receive power to "be my witnesses in Jerusalem, in all Judea and Samaria, and to the ends of the earth" (Acts 1:8). Acts 4 continues the story of the outpouring of the Spirit by telling how the followers of the risen Jesus are empowered to bear witness.

- Review Acts 4. What are the main themes of the disciples' message? How is their testimony described? Give examples of ways the disciples' bold witness is expressed in this text.
- Make a list of other important characters in this text and their responses to the disciples' witness.

2. One of the main story lines in Acts is the spread and growth of the movement called "the Way" throughout the Roman Empire, the ruling power at that time. This plot is driven by the conflict between the Spirit-power guiding the disciples and the power of the authorities.

 Notes

Notes

- In Acts 4, why do the Jewish authorities arrest Peter and the other disciples? What is at issue in this conflict?
- How do the disciples as leaders compare and contrast with the portrayal of the Jewish leadership in Acts 4? What are the distinguishing characteristics of both groups? What are their respective goals and objectives?
- How might the believers' claim that God alone is "sovereign Lord, who made the heaven and the earth, the sea, and everything in them" (4:24) cause conflict with the authorities?

3. A central theme throughout the Gospel of Luke and Acts is praise and prayer. Praise and prayer are ways of responding and relating to God through the power of expression.

- Why do the followers of Jesus praise God in Acts 4? Based on this, how would you describe their understanding of who God is and what God is doing?
- Note what the followers of Jesus pray for in Acts 4:24-30. Based on this prayer, describe their understanding of God and relationship with God.

4. Acts 4:32-37 provides another summary of the pattern of life in the community of Christ. Compare and contrast this portrait of community life in Christ with the one in Acts 2:42-47. What are the main emphases of the depiction in Acts 4:32-37?

Historical Context

1. The Romans destroyed the Jewish temple in Jerusalem in 70 C.E., before Acts was written. The destruction of the temple provides the historical context for the hope of Israel's restoration and the critique of Israel's leaders that is prominent throughout Luke and Acts. In Acts 4, Peter and the other disciples are arrested in the temple. The priestly aristocracy as well as the Sadducees and "rulers of the people and elders" (4:8) at this hearing also comprised the Jewish council that presided over Jesus' trial in the temple (Luke 22:66-71).

- How does knowing that the temple was destroyed affect the way you see the confrontation between the Jewish leaders' authority and the disciples, who are described as "uneducated and ordinary"? What lessons from history does this passage propose regarding leadership?
- Jews still lived under Roman rule at the time Acts was written. What does Acts 4 convey about how God will restore Israel and the nations and what that restoration might look like? What is significant about the fact that ordinary followers of Jesus led this restoration movement?

2. The account in Acts 4:32-37 of communal goods among the earliest followers of Jesus in Jerusalem draws on popular Greco-Roman notions of friendship at the time with the phrase "one heart and soul." It is also similar to descriptions of other Jewish groups. The *Rule of the Community*, from Qumran, an ancient settlement near the Dead Sea, indicates that the sharing of property and possessions was practiced by at least some groups in Palestinian Jewish culture.

• How much do you think this depiction of the community of Christ was influenced by Greco-Roman notions of friendship? How much do you think it describes the reality of common life together in Christ at that time?

• For a group in conflict with the authorities, there may have been additional reasons to share all goods in common. How might this vision of community be a response to strained social interactions or economic stress?

Lutheran Context

1. Martin Luther maintained that Christians are citizens of two kingdoms, a spiritual kingdom by which the Holy Spirit produces righteous people under Christ, and an earthly or temporal kingdom by which the wicked are restrained and outward peace is preserved. God works through both kingdoms, but these two reigns of God are different and not to be confused, as explained in an early document on Lutheran doctrine and practice:

> Christians, therefore, are obliged to be subject to political authority and to obey its commands and laws in all that may be done without sin. But if a command of the political authority cannot be followed without sin, one must obey God rather than any human beings (Acts 5:29). (The Augsburg Confession 16:6-7 [1530], in *The Book of Concord: The Confessions of the Evangelical Lutheran Church*, ed. Robert Kolb and Timothy J. Wengert [Augsburg Fortress, 2000], p. 50)

• When Peter and John are brought before the Jewish authorities, they are ordered "not to speak or teach at all in the name of Jesus" (4:18). Review their reply in Acts 4:19-20. How does this fit with the Lutheran concept of two kingdoms?

2. Luther's two kingdoms is a dynamic concept that says that obedience to all forms of human authority is never absolute, but always limited and conditional. If obeying human authority means disobedience to God, our allegiance to God must come first.

• When might we find the policies and practices of civil authorities in tension with God's purposes? As the community of Christ today, how do we go about discerning and responding to such tensions?

 Notes

Notes

• When the Jewish authorities apprehended the disciples, they "recognized [the disciples] as companions of Jesus" (4:13). How might others recognize that we have been with Jesus? Discuss whether being with Jesus shapes our manner of life in ways that are countercultural and at odds with the status quo today.

Devotional Context

1. In Acts 4 the disciples are mistreated and marginalized for their bold witness to Christ. In the face of harassment, believers pray to be bold in speaking God's word, and "they were all filled with the Holy Spirit and spoke the word of God with boldness" (Acts 4:31).

• Make a list of ways that you, your group, or your congregation might boldly witness to the power of the gospel of Jesus Christ today. If there are people being mistreated and marginalized in your area, how might you respond to those situations?

• Write a prayer reflecting challenges facing your community. Ask the Holy Spirit for guidance, wisdom, and boldness to bear witness to the power of the resurrection. Pray the prayer with your group.

Wrap-up

Be ready to look back over the work your group has done in this session.

Pray

Holy Spirit,
deliver us from just going through the motions
and help us heed your call.
Breathe into us the restlessness and courage
to do something new,
*   something saving,*
*   and something true,*
that we may be agents of your love and grace
and know in our bones what it means to be your people.
Through Jesus Christ our Lord. Amen.

Extending the Conversation

Homework

1. Read the next session's Bible text: Acts 8:1-40.

2. Make two columns on a sheet of paper. In one column make a list of the essential elements of living a successful life, from our culture's perspective. In the other column make a list of what is essential for you to live out your baptismal calling as a child of God. What are the

main differences between the two columns? How does trying to live out both of these visions cause tension?

Enrichment

1. If you wish to read through the entire book of Acts during this unit, read the following sections this week:

Day 1: Acts 5:1-16
Day 2: Acts 5:17-42
Day 3: Acts 6:1-15
Day 4: Acts 7:1-43
Day 5: Acts 7:44-60
Day 6: Acts 8:1-25
Day 7: Acts 8:26-40

2. Spend some time this week searching for examples of people who boldly bear witness to God's creative and redeeming power. These could be from news stories you read, movies you watch, or people you observe in the course of everyday life. Reflect on what makes for bold or courageous witness and what you find inspiring about it. Share your examples with the group at the next session.

3. Dig deeper into a topic such as the Roman Empire, the Jerusalem temple, or the Essene community in Qumran.

For Further Reading

Notes on Acts 4:1-37 in *Lutheran Study Bible, The HarperCollins Study Bible,* or *The New Oxford Annotated Bible.*

The Acts of the Apostles, by Luke Timothy Johnson, pp. 75-93.

To Every Nation under Heaven: The Acts of the Apostles, by Howard Clark Kee, pp. 61–74.

 Notes

Acts 8:1-40

Learner Session Guide

Focus Statement

After the stoning of Stephen and the ensuing persecution of believers, the Jesus movement spreads into other regions of Judea and Samaria, where the Spirit is already at work among those searching for God.

Key Verse

So Philip ran up to [the chariot] and heard [the Ethiopian] reading the prophet Isaiah. He asked, "Do you understand what you are reading?" He replied, "How can I, unless someone guides me?" And he invited Philip to get in and sit beside him. Acts 8:30-31

The Spirit on the Margins

⋰⋱ **Focus Image**

The Baptism of the Eunuch, 1641, Rembrandt van Rjin, Rosenwald Collection, Courtesy National Gallery of Art, Washington.

Gather

Check-in

Take this time to connect or reconnect with the others in your group and give a special welcome to newcomers. In the session Scripture text we begin to see the fulfillment of the words Jesus spoke before he ascended into heaven (Acts 1:8). After the martyrdom of a believer named Stephen, persecution of followers of Jesus results in expansion of the movement beyond Jerusalem and into Samaria, where Philip proclaims the gospel and baptizes Simon, a magician, and an Ethiopian eunuch.

Pray

Gracious and loving God of all peoples, empower us to bear witness to the good news of Jesus to those who inhabit the margins where they have been denied justice and search for understanding and hope. Cleanse our hearts and free our minds, that we may receive the gift of your Spirit and share it freely with those in need of your grace and help; in the name of the one who went about doing good and healing all who were oppressed. Amen.

Focus Activity

Think about the most memorable baptism you have seen. Who was there? What took place? What made this baptism memorable for you?

Open Scripture

Read Acts 8:1-40.

- As you listen to the passage with your heart, what words or phrases speak to you?

- How is the Spirit's activity described?

- What questions do you have?

 Notes

Join the Conversation

Literary Context

1. Acts 8 tells the story of how the community of Jesus' followers in Jerusalem became his "witnesses in Jerusalem, and in all Judea and Samaria, and to the end of the earth" (Acts 1:8). The impetus for this mission is a "severe persecution . . . against the church in Jerusalem" (8:1). Philip, one of seven men chosen to help distribute food (6:5), is the main character in Acts 8. Two pivotal characters in Acts, Stephen and Saul (later known as Paul), are also mentioned.

- The story in Acts 8 is preceded by an account of the martyrdom of Stephen, another of the seven appointed to distribute food. Read the conclusion of Stephen's speech to the council and the description of his death by stoning in Acts 7:44—8:1. What is your impression of Stephen? What effect would you expect Stephen's martyrdom to have on other followers of Jesus?

- The story in Acts 8 is followed by an account of Saul's conversion in Acts 9. Saul was present at Stephen's stoning (8:1) and persecuted believers in Jerusalem. His perspective changed when he encountered the risen Jesus on his way to the city of Damascus.

Notes

Read Acts 9:1-9. What is your impression of Saul at this point? How might Philip's preaching in Samaria and to the Ethiopian shed light on this story?

2. The first place the gospel of Christ is preached outside of Jerusalem is in Samaria (Acts 8:4-25). The Samaritans, half-siblings of the Jewish people, were on the fringe of Judaism. The mission to share the good news takes place first among marginal Jews, then among Gentiles (the Jewish term for everyone who is not a Jew).

• On the map on the next page, locate Jerusalem and Samaria.

• Reread Acts 8:5-13. What is the difference between the signs done by Philip and those done by Simon the magician?

• Reread Acts 8:14-25. Why did the Jerusalem church send Peter and John? Did Simon have a conversion? Give reasons for your response.

3. Before his ascension Jesus tells his followers they will be his witnesses "to the ends of the earth" (1:8). Ancient historians often identified Ethiopia with the ends of the earth. The Ethiopian in Acts 8 represents the outermost reaches of the Roman Empire, and as a eunuch he was also a marginal character. He is also portrayed as someone on the fringes of Judaism who is nonetheless on his way home from worshiping in Jerusalem.

• Philip meets the Ethiopian on the road from Jerusalem to Gaza. Find Gaza on the map on the next page.

• The Ethiopian is reading from the book of Isaiah (Isaiah 53:7-8 is quoted in Acts 8:32-33). Read Isaiah 53:1-9. Discuss how this passage sheds light on the exchange between Philip and the Ethiopian. Philip explains that the passage from Isaiah 53 is speaking of Christ. How might it also describe the Ethiopian's experience?

• Read Luke 24:13-27, which tells the story of Jesus on the road to Emmaus. In what ways is this story similar to the account of Philip and the Ethiopian?

4. Philip preaches the word to Simon and to the Ethiopian. Compare and contrast these two encounters. How are they similar and how are they different? What is Simon interested in? What is the Ethiopian looking for? How is the activity of the Spirit described in the two accounts?

Historical Context

1. Through the first seven chapters of Acts, the first followers of Jesus are a small community of Jews dwelling in Jerusalem and frequenting the temple. According to Acts, they begin to increase in number as Jews living around the Mediterranean Sea join in confessing Jesus as Messiah. This initial infusion of cultural diversity causes an internal

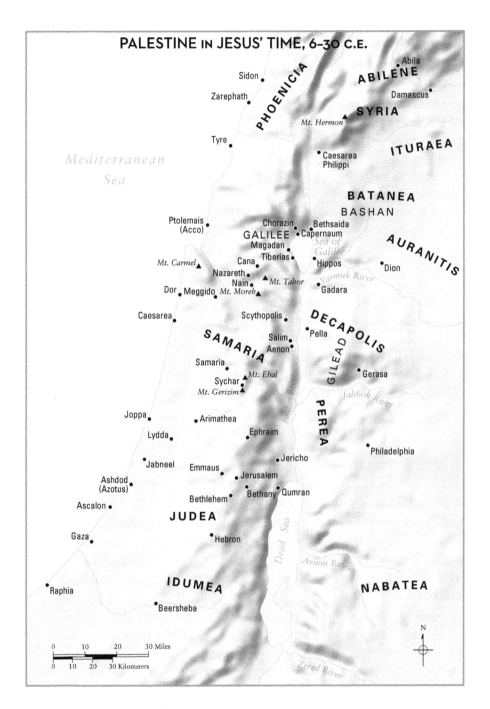

Notes

conflict between "Hellenistic Jews" from other areas, and "Hebrews" living in Judea (Acts 6:1-7). In Acts 8 persecution of the first community of believers, in Jerusalem, impels them farther out of what had been a relatively homogeneous cultural comfort zone and into a strange and wonderful multicultural world as Philip proclaims Christ to Simon and the Ethiopian. This is not yet a full-fledged mission to non-Jews or Gentiles, but rather a first foray to the margins of Judaism as a prelude to ministry in a world where idolatry was the norm.

Notes

• In *The Republic* Plato articulates the principle "Like always attracts like." This would seem to be true of most communities of faith, where people have shared beliefs but also tend to have similar cultural and socioeconomic backgrounds and even cultural traditions. In this respect, the story of the mission and expansion of the Jesus movement to the ends of the earth is counterintuitive, or contrary to the principle that "like attracts like." Review Philip's conversations with Simon and the Ethiopian. What can we learn about expanding the mission of Christ with those on the margins in our multicultural world? What are the motivations for doing this? What kind of qualities and skills are required? What kind of transformation can occur?

2. Sometimes the most intense conflicts are with those with whom we would seem to have the most in common. This is certainly true of the historic tension between Jews and Samaritans. Jewish and Samaritan sources offer different accounts of the origins of the Samaritans. However, Samaritan identity and practices were based on a Samaritan version of the Five Books of Moses, which was not very different from the version used in Judaism. The main difference was that the Samaritans worshiped on Mount Gerizim.

Luke has a special interest in Samaritans and emphasizes that Jesus mends the rift between Jews and Samaritans. In Luke's Gospel Samaritans are exemplars of faithfulness—in Jesus' parable of the good Samaritan (Luke 10:25-37) and in the one leper out of ten who returns to thank Jesus after his cleansing (Luke 17:11-19).

• Think about some inter-religious tensions that need to be healed today. Talk about how the good news of Jesus might be communicated and embodied in ways that promote reconciliation and also honor the ways God is active in different communities and traditions.

• Review Acts 8:14-17. Note that Peter and John go from Jerusalem to Samaria to pray for Samaritans who received the word of God to receive the Holy Spirit. Why do they do this? How does this differ from the Pentecost account of receiving the Spirit? What is significant about these differences?

Lutheran Context

1. The very foundation of Lutheran belief and practice is the priority of grace, that is, that everything, life itself, is pure gift. This is highlighted throughout the Gospel of Luke and Acts, with special emphasis on the Holy Spirit's presence in our experience of God's grace.

• Create a sketch or drawing of what your life would look like if you could give up your desire for power and yield to the Spirit's power, trusting that all is pure gift from God. What would it look like to do this as a group or a congregation? What are the risks of doing this?

2. Economics is also a focus throughout Luke–Acts. In contrast to God's eagerness to give unconditionally, we tend to calculate and give only with the expectation of some sort of return.

• Review Acts 8:18-20. Why does Simon the magician offer money for the gift of the Spirit? Why does Peter rebuff him? What happens when what is intended as gift becomes currency for exchange?

Devotional Context

1. The passage from Isaiah that the Ethiopian was reading is from Isaiah 53. Philip explains that the prophet Isaiah is speaking about Jesus and the humiliation and injustice he experienced. As a eunuch, the Ethiopian also would have experienced humiliation and perhaps injustice that may have caused him to resonate with Jesus. The emphasis, however, is not on common experiences of humiliation but rather on the "good news about Jesus" (8:35). The God of justice and love exonerated the Ethiopian and acclaimed him beloved.

• Review Acts 8:26-39. Reflect on a time when you or someone you know experienced humiliation, injustice, or other kinds of marginalization. How did you feel about this? How does the story of Philip and the Ethiopian speak to this experience?

• With a sense of urgency the Ethiopian seeks to be baptized. Through baptism we participate in Christ's death, so that we might be raised with him and walk in newness of life. Contemplate and discuss how through our baptism into Christ the Spirit breathes new life.

2. At the time Acts was written, Ethiopia would have been the limit of the known world, and a eunuch would have been regarded as a marginal human being. Philip's encounter with this man is a radical story of God's inclusive love and grace that know no boundaries.

• Look at the Focus Image, Rembrandt's drawing of this story. When this was drawn, Holland was heavily involved in the slave trade, and was also doing much missionary work to convert black Africans to the Christian faith. Compare and contrast the drawing with the story in Acts 8:26-40. How does the drawing convey the cultural assumptions and conventions of Rembrandt's time? How does it challenge those assumptions and conventions? Take a poll to find out whether members of your group think the drawing accurately depicts the story in Acts. What, if anything, would you change in the drawing?

Notes

Notes

Wrap-up

Be ready to look back over the work your group has done in this session.

Pray

O God, you have called your servants to ventures of which we cannot see the ending, by paths as yet untrodden, through perils unknown. Give us faith to go out with good courage, not knowing where we go, but only that your hand is leading us and your love supporting us; through Jesus Christ our Lord. (Evening Prayer, ELW p. 317)

Extending the Conversation

Homework

1. Read the next session's Bible text: Acts 10:1-48.

2. Role-play the Acts account of the meeting between Philip and Simon the magician and/or Philip and the Ethiopian eunuch. How would you enact these episodes in a contemporary context? Reflect on and discuss what these characters may have been like. What motivates them? What do you imagine they are thinking and feeling?

Enrichment

1. If you wish to read through the entire book of Acts during this unit, read the following sections this week:

Day 1: Acts 9:1-19a
Day 2: Acts 9:19b-31
Day 3: Acts 9:32-43
Day 4: Acts 10:1-8
Day 5: Acts 10:9-23a
Day 6: Acts 10:23b-33
Day 7: Acts 10:34-48

2. Simon is depicted as a person who practiced magic. Is it sometimes difficult to draw clear distinctions between beliefs and practices that are magical versus those that are religious? Interview a few people this week and ask them how or if they distinguish between faith and magic. How do they understand faith? How is it different from magic? Where do they see magical thinking at work in the church and the world? Where do they see faith at work in the church and the world?

3. Find out more about the persecution of early followers of Jesus and the effect this had on the spread of Christianity. Search for information online, in your church library, or at the local public

library. Consider sharing a brief summary of what you learn at one of the study sessions.

For Further Reading

Notes on Acts 8:1-40 in *Lutheran Study Bible*, *The HarperCollins Study Bible*, or *The New Oxford Annotated Bible*.

The Acts of the Apostles, by Luke Timothy Johnson.

Magic and Paganism in Early Christianity: The World of the Acts of the Apostles, by Hans-Josef Klauck. Minneapolis: Fortress, 2000, pp. 13-29.

Notes

Acts 10:1-48

Learner Session Guide

Focus Statement

Peter is led by the Spirit to the house of a righteous Gentile, Cornelius. When Cornelius receives the Spirit, he and Peter are both transformed and the first church consisting of both Jews and Gentiles is brought into being.

Key Verse

Then Peter began to speak to them: "I truly understand that God shows no partiality, but in every nation anyone who fears him and does what is right is acceptable to him." Acts 10:34-35

The Conversion of Peter

 Focus Image

Aphrodisias - Antique City. © iStockphoto.com / Maxime VIGE

Gather

Check-in

Take this time to connect or reconnect with the others in your group and give a special welcome to newcomers. Acts 10 tells about a pivotal turning point in the life of the Jesus movement. When Peter and the centurion Cornelius meet, both undergo conversions that affect how they see and behave with one another. This encounter signals the beginning of the mission to the Gentiles and sets in motion an ongoing process of discerning how Jews and Gentiles can live in relationship together as the people of God.

Pray

Creator of heaven and earth, we pray for open hearts and open minds to discern the ways your Spirit is at work in the world to bring people together. Stir our imaginations that we may see beyond borders and through barriers to acknowledge your impartiality. Deliver us from assumptions that keep us from recognizing those you have claimed as your own and from comfortable habits that hinder us from discovering your presence in those who are different. Make us part of your new creation. Amen.

Focus Activity

The Focus Image is an inscription from Aphrodisias, an important archaeological site in modern-day Turkey. "Godfearers" in Acts are Gentiles who had some relationship with the God of Abraham, Sarah, and Moses, and with the Jewish community. The first Gentile followers of Jesus were most likely Godfearers like Cornelius. Another inscription from Aphrodisias lists the names and occupations of some Gentile Godfearers:

> And the following Godfearers: Zenon, councillor, Tertullos, . . . Chrusippos, Gorgonios, bronze-smith, Tatianos, . . . tablet-maker, son of Attalos, Hortasios, stone-carver, Alexandros, boxer, Appianos, plasterer, Adolios, mincer, Zotikos, armband-maker, Zotikos, comedian, Eupithios, son of Eupithios, Patrikios, bronze-smith, Elpidianos, athlete, Heduchroos, Kallinikos, Balerianos, treasurer, Heuretos, son of Athenagoros, Paramonos, portrait-painter, Eutuchianos, fuller, Prokopios, money-changer . . .

These Gentile Godfearers were attracted to Judaism for a variety of reasons. They became full members of the community of Christ by being baptized and receiving the Spirit. They did not have to officially convert to Judaism first. Discuss what you think drew these Godfearers to Judaism, which by Gentile standards involved some strange customs. What is it about the way of life together in Christ that might interest and engage nonbelievers? Why are more people not drawn into the community of Christ?

 Notes

Notes

Open Scripture

Read Acts 10:1-48.

- As you listen to the passage with your heart, what words or phrases speak to you?

- What images come to mind as you hear this passage?

- What character in the story is most like you?

Join the Conversation

Literary Context

1. The story of Cornelius marks the beginning of the mission to the Gentiles. Both Cornelius and Peter receive revelations in the form of visions that provide divine guidance in this new phase of God's mission. The visions reveal God's purpose as well as how Cornelius and Peter must cooperate with what the Spirit is doing.

- When Jesus was brought to the temple as a child, a Jew by the name of Simeon took him in his arms and blessed him. Read about this encounter in Luke 2:25-32. In what ways are Simeon's words about Jesus fulfilled in the story of Cornelius?

- Read the description of Cornelius's vision in Acts 10:1-8. Act out this scene or imagine that you are the director for this scene in a movie or play. How do you think Cornelius should be portrayed? How will the angel appear, and what tone of voice do you want the angel to use? How quickly does Cornelius respond? What is the most important thing for viewers to take away from this scene?

- Read the description of Peter's vision in Acts 10:9-16. Again, act out this scene or imagine that you are the director for this scene in a movie or play. How do you think Paul should be portrayed? How will you show this vision? What tone should the voice in 10:13 use? What tone of voice should Peter use? What is the most important thing for viewers to take away from this scene?

 Notes

2. In Acts the first of three accounts of Paul's conversion precedes the meeting between Cornelius and Peter. Paul, originally called Saul, is described as a religious fanatic who was apprehending followers of Jesus and taking them to Jerusalem. In session 3 we learned that he was present at Stephen's stoning and death. Both Paul and Peter undergo conversions as they are required to reckon with their prejudice against Gentiles and revise their perception of what God is doing.

• Read the account of Paul's conversion in Acts 9:1-19a. Compare and contrast the description of Paul's conversion with the account of Peter's conversion in Acts 10:9-23. How are the circumstances of Paul's conversion different from Peter's? What in particular about Paul's perspective changes? What in particular about Peter's perspective changes?

• What do Acts 9:1-19a and 10:9-23 reveal about what is at issue in including Gentiles in the community of Christ? List any assumptions you have about Paul's reasons for persecuting Jesus' followers in Jerusalem and about points of contention between Jews and Gentiles. How are your assumptions confirmed or challenged by these passages?

3. Cornelius the centurion is an important character in Luke–Acts because he is the first Gentile convert. He is also a Roman military officer in Caesarea, a port city built by Herod the Great and named Caesarea in honor of the Roman emperor, Caesar Augustus. Centurions feature prominently in the Gospel of Luke and Acts. The depiction of Cornelius in Acts 10 bears a resemblance to the centurion in Luke 7:1-10, who is also described as having a favorable relationship with the Jewish community.

• Locate Caesarea on the map on page 61, and note its prime location along the Mediterranean Sea.

• Read Luke 7:1-10 and compare the portraits of the two centurions. What is significant about the parallels between the centurion in Luke 7 and Cornelius? Would you expect these two Roman military leaders to be portrayed in such a favorable light? Why or why not? As centurions these two men represent the Roman Empire. Discuss what kind of challenge this poses for followers of Jesus.

• Use the details provided in Acts 10 and your imagination to develop a character sketch of Cornelius. What kind of person is he? Why is he interested in Judaism? What does it mean for him to live as a centurion and a Godfearer in the Roman Empire? Describe

Notes

the tensions or conflicts that might arise for him because of his connection to God and the people of God.

4. As the story unfolds, Peter goes to Cornelius's house and explains to everyone in the household that he came because "God has shown me that I should not call anyone profane or unclean" (10:28). He then asks why Cornelius has sent for him. After Cornelius recounts his vision, Peter gives an important speech.

• Review Peter's speech in Acts 10:34-43. Identify the main themes and what Peter emphasizes about God and Jesus. How does Peter's version of the gospel of Jesus Christ in this passage compare with your understanding of the gospel?

• Read Acts 10:44-48. How do the claims that "God shows no partiality" (10:34) and Jesus Christ is Lord of all affect Peter and Cornelius? In what ways does each person stay the same, and how are they changed?

Historical Context

1. Jews often interacted with Gentiles in the course of daily life without any misgivings. Nonetheless, their belief in one and only one God caused Jews to regard Gentiles as idolaters and therefore as sinners. This posed problems for Jews because meals and hospitality, featured prominently in Luke–Acts, were among the most important social occasions in antiquity. Gentiles would pour out libations to the gods at meals, and Jewish food laws made it difficult for Jews and Gentiles to share the same table. The risen Lord's command to Peter to "kill and eat" the animals seen in the vision does not resolve the issue conclusively (see Acts 15). The purity laws pertaining to food are not abolished here but suspended for a particular purpose. This episode sets in motion an ongoing process of negotiation and compromise between Jewish and Gentile believers.

• Judaism has often been characterized as a religion based on a strict interpretation of the law from which Jesus delivered people. However, Jesus was a Jew who observed the law, and so were his Jewish followers. What are some assumptions or even prejudices you have about Jewish purity laws, and how are they challenged by this passage?

• Although Jews had scruples about idolatry and table fellowship with Gentiles, there were a number of Gentiles, like Cornelius, who were drawn to Judaism. Why do you imagine Cornelius was involved in the Jewish community? What particular beliefs and practices do you think he found compelling?

2. In his sermon in Acts 10:34-43 Peter makes a bold claim when he calls Jesus Christ the Lord of all. The Greek text specifies *"this one* is Lord of all" (10:36), suggesting that Peter is countering the claims of the time that the Roman emperor was "lord." The lordship of Roman emperors had to do with the military force with which they obtained and preserved the *Pax Romana* or "peace," another word used in 10:36.

- How do you react to Peter's claiming Jesus Christ as Lord of all while he was speaking in the household of the Roman centurion Cornelius?

- How does this historical background affect your understanding of what it means to declare Jesus as Lord? How might you communicate this today in words or images?

Lutheran Context

1. Lutherans emphasize baptism as a primary means of experiencing God's grace and often associate receiving the Spirit with baptism. In the session Scripture text and others in Acts, however, hearing the word is the occasion for an outpouring of the Spirit. The episode in Acts 10 concludes with the Holy Spirit falling on all who heard the word (10:44), and then those who had received the gift of the Spirit were baptized (10:47-48). The Lutheran theological understanding of the importance of both Word and Sacrament may shed some light on this. Lutherans affirm that God continues to speak through the Scriptures, but also that the Scriptures need to be interpreted in the light of Christ, who is the eternal Word of God. In Acts the Holy Spirit works through the Word and baptism as a means of grace in profound and surprising ways.

- How do you understand the relationship of the Spirit, the Word, and baptism in Acts 10? How do you experience the Spirit through the Word and baptism in your own life?

- In what ways is the experience of God's grace in Acts 10 surprising and unsettling? How does the experience of God's grace through the power of the Spirit affirm and restore life? How have you experienced God's grace as both unsettling and affirming or life-giving?

Devotional Context

1. Acts succinctly describes the devotional life or spirituality of Cornelius in this way: "He was a devout man who feared God with all his household; he gave alms generously to the people and prayed constantly to God" (10:2). It is not uncommon to think about devotional life as prayer, but it is less common to regard almsgiving or sharing resources with others as a spiritual practice.

 Notes

Notes

There are a variety of spiritual practices as well as many different spiritual temperaments. Devotional or spiritual practices can include both contemplation and action, knowledge and experience, and community and solitude. Acts can help to broaden and deepen our understanding and practice of spirituality.

- Reflect on and discuss which of the following best describes your way of approaching prayer:
  - ❑ Words express poetic praise; I ask for knowledge and guidance.
  - ❑ Let words and feelings evoke God's presence in this moment.
  - ❑ Empty the mind of distractions and simply *be* in the presence of the Holy.
  - ❑ My life and my work are my prayer.
- Reflect on and discuss which of the following best describes your devotion or spirituality in action:
  - ❑ It is important that I fulfill my vocation (calling) in the world.
  - ❑ It is important that I learn to walk in holiness with the Lord.
  - ❑ It is important that I be one with the Creator.
  - ❑ It is important that I obey God's will completely.

Wrap-up

Be ready to look back over the work your group has done in this session.

Pray

Lord of heaven and earth, grant us the grace to trust your Spirit moving in us and through us, crossing boundaries to build bridges and bring peace. Give us the vision to see others as you see them and to bear witness in word and deed to the one who went about doing good and healing all who were oppressed. Through Jesus Christ our Lord. Amen.

Extending the Conversation

Homework

1. Read the next session's Bible text: Acts 17:1-34.

2. Do an improvisational skit of the meeting between Cornelius and Peter.

Enrichment

1. If you wish to read through the entire book of Acts during this unit, read the following sections this week:

Day 1: Acts 11:1-30
Day 2: Acts 12:1-25
Day 3: Acts 13:1-52
Day 4: Acts 14:1-28
Day 5: Acts 15:1-41
Day 6: Acts 16:1-40
Day 7: Acts 17:1-34

2. Although we don't follow Jewish purity laws, every culture has purity codes of one kind or another. While purity codes serve to bring order out of perceived disorder, they also erect boundaries, because the disorder is seen as a danger or threat. In our culture, for example, the phrase "the other side of the tracks" connotes a boundary of social acceptability. As you go through the week, note examples of cultural or religious "purity codes" that differentiate between order and disorder. What are some of the positive and negative effects of these codes?

For Further Reading

Notes on Acts 10:1-48 in *Lutheran Study Bible, The HarperCollins Study Bible,* or *The New Oxford Annotated Bible.*

The Acts of the Apostles, by Luke Timothy Johnson.

Magic and Paganism in Early Christianity: The World of the Acts of the Apostles, by Hans-Josef Klauck, pp. 31–44.

 Notes

Acts 17:1-34

Learner Session Guide

Focus Statement

In Paul's proclamation of Christ, nonbelievers see political implications and disruptions to civic life. Paul's mission strategy is to look for common denominators as points of contact, but also to interpret the Scriptures and challenge idolatry.

Key Verse

They dragged Jason and some believers before the city authorities, shouting, "These people who have been turning the world upside down have come here also, and Jason has entertained them as guests. They are all acting contrary to the decrees of the emperor, saying that there is another king named Jesus." Acts 17:6-7

World Upside Down

⋅꙳⋅ Focus Image

Saint Paul Preaching at Athens. Universal Images Group / SuperStock

Gather

Check-in

Take this time to connect or reconnect with the others in your group and give a special welcome to newcomers. We continue our study in Acts 17, but a lot has happened since the Spirit-infused meeting between Peter and Cornelius. James, the brother of Jesus and leader of the Jerusalem church, has been executed by King Herod. Peter has been arrested and then delivered from prison. Paul and Barnabas have been sent out from their home congregation in Antioch to proclaim the gospel. The focus of Acts now shifts to their mission as it moves westward into Greece and then ultimately to Rome, and ever more deeply into a Gentile culture that is characterized by idolatry.

Pray

Beloved and sovereign God, through the death and resurrection of your Son you bring us into your kingdom of justice and mercy. By your Spirit, give us your wisdom, that we may treasure the life that comes from Jesus Christ, our Savior and Lord. Amen.

Focus Activity

The Focus Image is Raphael's rendering of Paul preaching in Athens. Observe the painting and identify the features that indicate the public and political nature of Paul's message and mission. In many places in the world today, faith has become a more private and personal matter. Reflect on why this may be the case. What are Christians called to be and do in the public square?

Open Scripture

Read Acts 17:1-34.

- As you listen to the passage with your heart, what words or phrases speak to you?

- What thoughts or feelings does this passage evoke in you?

- What is being turned upside down?

Notes

Join the Conversation

Literary Context

1. The mission to the Gentiles is in full swing as Paul arrives in Greece. One of the recurring themes in Acts since the martyrdom of Stephen is resistance to and reaction against the gospel message that God raised from the dead Jesus of Galilee—who was executed as an enemy of the Roman order—and made him both "Lord" and "Christ." In Acts 17 we see that Jews and Gentiles oppose this message, for different reasons.

- Read Acts 17:1-9, the account of Paul speaking the gospel of Christ to Jews in the synagogue at Thessalonica. What is Paul's strategy for or approach to sharing the good news here? How do the Jews in Thessalonica respond? Identify their objections to Paul's message and their reasons for being jealous. What do you think about these criticisms of Paul and his message?

Notes

- Read Acts 17:16-34, the account of Paul speaking publicly in Athens to an educated and philosophically oriented Gentile audience. Compare and contrast how Paul delivers the message of Christ in Athens and in the synagogue at Thessalonica. What is Paul's strategy and message in Athens? Identify the objections to Paul's message and his response. What do you think about these criticisms of Paul's message?

- Turn to the map on page 61 and trace the expansion and growth of the early Christian movement as described in Acts. Start in Jerusalem, move north to the city of Antioch in modern-day Syria, and then follow along the southern coast of modern-day Turkey. In this session's Scripture text, the movement expands into Greece with Paul's visits to Thessalonica and Athens.

2. In the ancient world idols were made to represent an alleged deity or god. To curry favor with the gods, people built temples, made sacrifices, and performed rituals. Idolatry, the worship of idols, was the main challenge to bringing the good news of Jesus to Gentile audiences. While Cornelius and some other Gentiles were Godfearers familiar with the one God of the Jews, the situation was different in the public square in Greece. As Paul entered Athens, Acts reports, "he was deeply distressed to see that the city was full of idols" (Acts 17:16).

- Martin Luther said that whatever we place our trust in and cling to is our God. He identified money and possessions as the most common idols. What do you think about this? What idols do you see in the world today? How does the gospel of Christ speak to modern expressions of idolatry?

- Make a list of some of the problems and adverse effects of idolatry, whether in ancient or modern times. How does the message about Christ's death and resurrection speak to these issues?

3. In the synagogue Paul reads the Scriptures with fellow Jews to show them that Jesus is the Messiah awaited by the Jewish people (Acts 17:2-3). However, in the public square Paul cannot assume that his audience knows or cares about Jewish Scriptures. In speaking the gospel message here, Paul leverages the audience's philosophical frame of reference.

- Some of Paul's listeners are Stoics, followers of an ancient philosophical tradition that held, among other things, that God is revealed in nature. In contrast, in the Bible God is often hidden until revealed through actions or revelations. Review Acts 17:22-31 and list some ways that Paul attempts to connect with his Stoic listeners.

- Today there is often tension between a scientific worldview and faith perspectives. How might people of faith take a cue from this text to have more constructive conversations with science?

• What do you think about Paul's attempts to connect with his audience? What are some strengths and limitations in our efforts today to find common ground between ourselves and people we want to reach with the gospel of Christ?

Historical Context

1. The connection between religion and politics in the ancient world and Roman Empire was strong. Local religious cults were an integral part of the fabric of society. Honoring and sacrificing to patron gods was thought to favorably predispose them toward the city. The Roman emperor also was worshiped in most cities. These religious traditions and practices were believed to lend stability to society.

What distinguished the Jews as a people was the firm conviction that the God of Abraham, Moses, and the prophets was the sovereign creator of the universe and the one God to whom they pledged loyalty. Paul and other followers of Christ not only believed in this creator; they claimed that this one God raised from the dead Jesus, who had been executed as an enemy of the Roman order.

• Review Acts 17. In what ways were Paul and other believers turning the world—as people knew it—"upside down" (17:6)?

• List some recent examples of groups, societies, or nations in which religion has been a stabilizing force. What are the drawbacks of this? In what sorts of situations would you say that individual Christians or congregations are called to turn the world upside down?

2. The Epicureans and Stoics mentioned in Acts followed two important philosophical schools of thought. Both had teaching institutes in Athens. Although there were differences between the two groups, both focused on practical matters and how to lead the good life, and specialized in an ancient form of what would now be called pastoral care. In ancient times philosophers also engaged in discussions about ethics, or how to live.

• Review Acts 17:22-31 and identify both what Paul's sermon has in common with these philosophical traditions and what is distinctive about Paul's message.

• Reflect on the gospel message and other forms of spirituality or self-help traditions in the world today. What are some points of contact? What are some differences?

Lutheran Context

1. Martin Luther's study of the Bible led to the insight that God's grace, blessings, and saving actions come to us as gifts. This happens because of what God has done through Christ's life, death, and

 Notes

Notes

resurrection, not because of anything we do. In contrast, ancient people were caught up in trying to minimize life's hardships and perhaps ward off evil by performing what seemed to them the proper rituals to appease the wrath of the gods and win their approval.

• Where in Paul's sermon in Acts 17:22-31 do you find references or allusions to God's grace? Discuss why people who worshiped idols might have difficulties with these words of grace. What makes these words difficult for people today?

• Reread Acts 17:30-31 and talk about how God's grace is experienced in the call to repentance and the promise that God will judge the world in righteousness.

2. The emphasis on God's grace is an integral part of Lutheran theology and understandings of God. However, there are often inconsistencies between the "official" theology we profess and our working beliefs. (For example, think of some of the things we say without thinking, such as "There's no such thing as a free lunch.") Deeply embedded within us, these working beliefs are not always centered on an image of a loving and gracious God.

• Take a few moments to reflect on and discuss this with one another. What is your underlying image of God? What is your underlying image of yourself? What changes in your beliefs and practices would put more emphasis on God's grace and the good news of Christ?

Devotional Context

1. People in the ancient world perceived and experienced the world and themselves much differently than we do. They lived in a world filled with gods, deities, spirits, demons, and other external forces—some friendly and others hostile—that they believed could impact the quality of their lives. As philosopher Charles Taylor observes, "Living in the enchanted, porous world of our ancestors was inherently living socially" (*A Secular Age*, Harvard University Press, 2007). In contrast, he describes our "secular age" as a disenchanted world in which thoughts, feelings, and spirituality are personal, internal matters. This results in what Taylor calls the bounded or "buffered self." We see ourselves as in control and masters of our own meanings and fate.

• Do some writing on how you see yourself and God. Who or what is in charge in your life?

• Reflect on what we can learn from Acts about our personal experiences of faith and opening up the "buffered self." How might our devotional lives be shared with one another and the world?

Wrap-up

Be ready to look back over the work your group has done in this session.

Notes

Pray

Teach us your ways, Lord, that we may be swept up in worship with the saints, which surges in wonder, gratitude, and obedience and shapes our lives into an irrepressible YES to you, to all our sisters and brothers, and to the presence of the kingdom among us. (adapted from *Guerrillas of Grace: Prayers for the Battle,* by Ted Loder, twentieth anniversary ed., Augsburg, 2004)

Extending the Conversation

Homework

1. Read the next session's Bible text: Acts 19:1-41.

2. Make a list of what in our culture could be defined as idolatry. Include as many things as you can. What makes these things idolatrous? What is their attraction? How does idolatry affect our awareness of and relation to the living God?

Enrichment

1. If you wish to read through the entire book of Acts during this unit, read the following sections this week:

Day 1: Acts 18:1-17
Day 2: Acts 18:18-28
Day 3: Acts 19:1-10
Day 4: Acts 19:11-20
Day 5: Acts 19:21-27
Day 6: Acts 19:28-36
Day 7: Acts 19:37-41

2. As you go through the week, observe and note any rituals or acts of devotion that convey faith or trust. What is the purpose of these acts? What understandings of God and self are implied? Compare and contrast what you observe with your understanding of what it means to live as a Christian.

For Further Reading

Notes on Acts 17:1-34 in *Lutheran Study Bible, The HarperCollins Study Bible,* or *The New Oxford Annotated Bible.*

The Acts of the Apostles, by Luke Timothy Johnson, pp. 304–320.

Magic and Paganism in Early Christianity: The World of the Acts of the Apostles, by Hans-Josef Klauck, pp. 73–95.

Acts 19:1-41

Focus Statement

On his second missionary journey, Paul goes to Ephesus, the capital of Asia Minor, where he causes another disturbance by calling into question the practice of magic and the local goddess Artemis. The threat of economic loss is the underlying cause of this disturbance.

Key Verse

These he gathered together, with the workers of the same trade, and said, "Men, you know that we get our wealth from this business. You also see and hear that not only in Ephesus but in almost the whole of Asia this Paul has persuaded and drawn away a considerable number of people by saying that gods made with hands are not gods." Acts 19:25-26

A Riot in Ephesus

⋰⋱ **Focus Image**

Bull. ©iStockphoto.com / ginosphotos

Gather

Check-in

Take this time to connect or reconnect with the others in your group and give a special welcome to newcomers. As we continue our study of Acts, we join Paul in Ephesus, a city at its peak in the first century, when it became the capital of Asia Minor. It was also a commercial center and home to the Temple of Artemis, one of the ancient world's seven wonders. In a dramatic episode in Acts 19, a confrontation between Paul and silversmith Demetrius challenges the idolatry woven into the very fabric of social life, exposes the economic underpinnings of religious life, and clarifies the countercultural nature of the community of Christ.

Pray

Creator and source of all life, empower us through the power of the Holy Spirit to recognize the false idols that deform our hopes and desires, that we may trust your goodness and grace and walk in the newness of life you grant us through Jesus Christ our Lord. Amen.

Focus Activity

As they traveled from Egypt to the promised land, the ancient Israelites created a god for themselves, a golden calf. Look at the Focus Image. What does it represent? As you contemplate the image, discuss what kinds of gods we create for ourselves today. How do these idols affect us, others, and the world?

Open Scripture

Read Acts 19:1-41.

- As you listen to the passage with your heart, what words or phrases speak to you?

- How would you describe the disturbance in Ephesus?

- How would you describe Paul, based on this passage?

Join the Conversation

Literary Context

1. Paul's mission is now the central focus in Acts and will remain so to the end. The Acts 19 account of his two-year stay in Ephesus reflects Paul's mission strategy. As in Acts 17, we see Paul first in a synagogue engaging fellow Jews in discussions about Jesus, and then proclaiming the gospel in a public square. The synagogue and the public square are two very different cultural settings with very different audiences, but Paul adapts his message and evokes different responses in these two contexts.

- Locate Ephesus on the map on page 61.

- Read Acts 19:1-20 and identify the Jews Paul interacts with. What is Paul's message in the synagogue, and how is it received? How do the Jewish exorcists engage with Paul's ministry in Ephesus, and what impact does it have on the audience?

- Read Acts 19:21-41 and describe the civic unrest that ensued as a consequence of Paul's preaching in the public square. What does Paul say that the silversmith Demetrius finds so disturbing? What are the underlying reasons for his reaction to Paul's message? What are the accusations against Paul, and how are they handled?

2. Although Acts 11:26 says that "it was in Antioch that the disciples were first called 'Christians,'" the preferred designation for the Jesus movement in Acts is "the Way." *Christian* was a label ascribed to followers of Jesus by the Romans. It simply meant one associated with Christ, while the Way implied a particular form or pattern of life characteristic of a movement. This expression is first introduced in Luke 3:4 regarding John the Baptist: "The voice of one crying out in the wilderness: 'Prepare the way of the Lord, make his paths straight'" (see also Isaiah 40:3).

• Considering your reading of Acts so far, how would you describe the distinctive pattern of life for followers of the Way? (It may help to look again at the brief descriptions in Acts 2:43-47 and 4:32-37, and passages in which the phrase "the Way" occurs, such as Acts 9:2; 18:25; 22:4; and especially 24:14-21.) What points of tension or conflict do you see between this pattern of life and that of those who worshiped Greco-Roman gods?

• Today Christians tend to talk about their faith as what they believe rather than what they do, but the opposite was the case in antiquity. What are the most important practices of the Christian faith? In what ways are core Christian beliefs and practices in tension with the dominant culture today?

3. The writer of Luke–Acts devotes more attention to economic matters than any other New Testament writer. The theme of poverty and wealth is first introduced in Mary's song, which claims that God "has filled the hungry with good things, and sent the rich away empty" (Luke 1:53). In his inaugural sermon Jesus announces that he has been sent "to bring good news to the poor, . . . to proclaim release to the captives and recovery of sight to the blind, to let the oppressed go free, to proclaim the year of the Lord's favor" (Luke 4:18-19).

The controversy in Ephesus exposes the inextricable connection between religion and economics in antiquity. Ephesus was home to a famous temple to the goddess Artemis, and silversmiths like Demetrius made money by selling shrines honoring her. While a select few profited from the practice of idolatry, 90 percent of the population barely had enough to survive.

• Review Acts 19:21-41. Compare and contrast the economics of the Artemis cult with the description of the community of Christ in Acts 2:43-45 and 4:32-37. What might have been attractive to nonbelievers as they observed the community of Christ's way of life? How does this way of life together in Christ challenge assumptions, habits, and practices characteristic of our way of life?

• In the Gospel of Luke, as in Judaism, idolatry is associated with greed. At one point Jesus tells his followers: "No slave can serve two masters; for a slave will either hate the one and love the other, or be devoted to the one and despise the other. You cannot serve God and wealth" (Luke 16:13). How does this shed light on Acts 19:21-41? In light of the teachings on wealth and greed in Luke–Acts, and the large number of people living at subsistence levels in today's world, talk about how you think Christians and the church should handle economic matters.

4. The reaction to Paul's ministry in Ephesus highlights a major issue in Acts: Why does a movement affirming that God is impartial and preaching peace through Jesus Christ (Acts 10:34-36) meet with such resistance? Even as the movement gains followers, the good news about Christ and demonstrations of Spirit-power disturb the status quo and arouse hostility and dissension in both synagogue and city. As we continue our study of Acts, we will see this conflict intensify. Ultimately, Paul will be sent to Rome and put on trial.

• What about the Way would have been challenging or disruptive for religious and state authorities? Talk about how life would have changed for those who became followers of Jesus. Is it possible to have this kind of transformation without tension or conflict?

• The ancient world was organized around public devotion to the gods. The economy and social life revolved around rituals, festivals, temples, and so on, all geared to gain the favor and protection of the gods. All of this was aimed at bending fate (believed to be dictated by the gods) to favor the city and individual devotees. How did the perspective of the followers of Jesus differ from this dominant worldview? How do Christian perspectives on the world, life, meaning, and purpose differ from dominant cultural perspectives today?

Historical Context

1. Acts 19:11-20 contrasts the experience of the Spirit's power with the ancient practice of magic, depicted as incompatible with the Way. Gentiles and Jews practiced magic in the ancient world, and Ephesus was a major center of this practice in Asia Minor. Specific words or phrases were used in performing magical acts in efforts to manipulate spiritual beings. Jewish priests were believed to know the divine names and use them in exorcisms. This is probably why the Jewish exorcists in Acts 19:13-16 "tried to use the name of the Lord Jesus over those who had evil spirits." This episode shows that it is not possible to invoke the name of Jesus to hold sway over evil spirits without being a follower of Jesus, his teachings, and his example. Remarkably, Acts reports that after the failure of the seven sons of the Jewish priest named Sceva, "many of those who became believers confessed and

Notes

Notes

disclosed their practices. A number of those who practiced magic collected their books and burned them publicly" (19:18-19). The books referred to here would have recorded magical incantations. In that era it was not uncommon to burn books seen as dangerous or subversive.

• Why did these new believers feel compelled to burn their books? Talk about the difference between the power of the Spirit and the power of magic.

• Brainstorm examples of popular religious practices today that include magical thinking.

2. Paul's ability to read and adapt to different cultural contexts and situations is one of his more remarkable skills and an integral part of his mission strategy. In the synagogue he is a Jew interpreting Scripture and debating with other Jews. Outside the synagogue, where people have little knowledge about Judaism, he is portrayed as a philosopher and public speaker trying to persuade an audience, using Greco-Roman cultural idioms and conventions to communicate the gospel.

• What wisdom from Paul's mission strategy could we apply to the church's mission? How does the church convey the countercultural message of the gospel of Jesus Christ in ways that engage people in today's world? How do you imagine Paul might have adapted his mission strategy in our cultural contexts?

Lutheran Context

1. The problem of idolatry is a key issue not only for Paul, but also in the Old Testament, Judaism, and Luther's theology. Idolatry is prohibited in the first commandment (Exodus 20:4-6; Deuteronomy 5:8-10) and in the Shema, the central statement of Jewish faith: "Hear, O Israel: The LORD is our God, the LORD alone. You shall love the LORD your God with all your heart, and with all your soul, and with all your might" (Deuteronomy 6:4-5).

• In Scripture God is described as having an exclusive claim on our love, trust, and obedience. In our life and faith today, what are some things that stand in the way of giving our love, trust, and obedience to God?

• In the Bible and in the theological tradition, idolatry is seen to be the underlying cause of sin. What are some of the ways that putting our trust in anything or anyone other than God diminishes the quality of life for ourselves or others? Give some concrete examples of how this kind of idolatry leads to sin.

Devotional Context

1. Devotion and the desires of the heart are at the crux of any discussion of idolatry and faithfulness to God. Many other things compete for our attention and are the object of our desires. For the most part, our desires are the same as the desires of others. We want what others have, what the culture tells us we should want. Growing in our love and trust of God, then, requires us to recognize how our devotion and desires have been deformed and turned inward on ourselves—so that we can instead direct them to God and God's purposes.

- Make a list or draw a sketch of things you desire and to which you are devoted. Reflect on the sources and motivations for your desires and devotion. Which desires and devotions would you like to reform in light of your faith commitments? How might you do that?

- Write about what it means for you to love and trust God with your whole heart. How is your trust and love of God shown in the way you live your life and relate to others?

Wrap-up

Be ready to look back over the work your group has done in this session.

Pray

Eternal One, Silence from whom our words come, Questioner from whom our questions arise, Lover to whom all our loves hint, Disturber in whom we find our rest; startle us with your presence, renew us through your power, and ground us in your grace. Amen.

Extending the Conversation

Homework

1. Read the next session's Bible text: Acts 24:1-27.

2. Think about advertisements on TV and in other media and how they condition human desire and devotion. How do they influence people into wanting certain things? Why are they so effective?

 Notes

Notes

Enrichment

1. If you wish to read through the entire book of Acts during this unit, read the following sections this week:

Day 1: Acts 20:1-16
Day 2: Acts 20:17-38
Day 3: Acts 21:1-26
Day 4: Acts 21:27-40
Day 5: Acts 22:1-30
Day 6: Acts 23:1-35
Day 7: Acts 24:1-27

2. As you go through the week, observe and note the various mission strategies you see enacted by the church and other institutions. What are some differences between how the church does mission and how businesses pursue their missions? Is there anything the church can learn from business models? How do these various mission strategies challenge the culture, and how do they adapt to it?

For Further Reading

Notes on Acts 19:1-41 in *Lutheran Study Bible, The HarperCollins Study Bible,* or *The New Oxford Annotated Bible.*

The Acts of the Apostles, by Luke Timothy Johnson, pp. 336–353.

Magic and Paganism in Early Christianity: The World of the Acts of the Apostles, by Hans-Josef Klauck, pp. 97–110.

Acts 24:1-27

Learner Session Guide

Focus Statement

In the second half of Acts, Paul travels throughout the Roman Empire proclaiming the good news of Jesus Christ to Jews and Gentiles. He encounters much resistance and on several occasions finds himself in prison. In Caesarea he explains to Jewish and Roman authorities that he is on trial for the resurrection.

Key Verse

"Or let these men here tell what crime they had found when I stood before the council, unless it was this one sentence that I called out while standing before them, 'It is about the resurrection of the dead that I am on trial before you today.'"
Acts 24:20-21

On Trial for the Resurrection

◌⁖◌ Focus Image

In the *Harrowing of Hades* fresco in the Chora Church, Istanbul, c. 1315, raising Adam and Eve is depicted as part of the Resurrection icon, as it always is in the East. © José Luiz Bernardes Ribeiro / CC-BY-SA-3.0

Gather

Check-in

Take this time to connect or reconnect with the others in your group and give a special welcome to newcomers. After the uproar in Ephesus, Paul continues to Macedonia and Greece, then to Troas and Miletus in Asia Minor, where he announces, "And now, as a captive to the Spirit, I am on my way to Jerusalem, not knowing what will happen to me there, except that the Holy Spirit testifies to me in every city that imprisonment and persecutions are waiting for me" (Acts 20:22-23). Paul travels to Jerusalem next, but his presence there causes a controversy. He is sent to Caesarea, where the session Scripture text picks up the story as Paul defends himself before the Roman governor Felix. Paul is now prisoner on trial in the Roman judicial system for a theological dispute with fellow Jews about the resurrection.

Pray

Risen Lord, make us faithful followers of the Spirit of your resurrection. Grant that we may be inwardly renewed; dying to ourselves that you may live in us and through us. May our lives serve as signs of the transforming power of your love, that we may join

Notes

together with you in the ongoing work of the renewal and redemption of all creation. Amen.

Focus Activity

The Focus Image is a fresco in the Chora Church in Istanbul, Turkey, that depicts the risen Jesus pulling Adam and Eve out of hell. This is the most common artistic representation of the resurrection in the Eastern Orthodox Church. Create your own sketch, picture, or painting of Jesus' resurrection. What are the similarities and differences between your image of resurrection and the Focus Image?

Open Scripture

Read Acts 24:1-27.

- As you listen to the passage with your heart, what words or phrases speak to you?

- What thoughts and emotions does this passage raise for you?

- How would you describe Paul here?

Join the Conversation

Literary Context

1. The mission that began in Jerusalem on Pentecost continues to expand. In Acts 19, the Scripture text for session 6, Paul was in Ephesus proclaiming the gospel. He moves on from there to Macedonia, Greece, Troas, and Miletus. After ongoing debate and dispute about Jesus with Jewish leaders in the synagogues throughout Asia and Greece, Paul returns to Jerusalem. In Acts 24, the Jewish leaders in Jerusalem send Paul to Rome (by way of Caesarea) to be tried and ultimately executed.

• On the map on page 61, trace the expansion and growth of the Jesus movement from Jerusalem, the symbolic center of Judaism, to Rome, the seat of the Roman Empire.

 Notes

2. A large narrative section in Acts begins with Paul's arrival in Jerusalem (21:17) and ends with him under house arrest in Rome "testifying to the kingdom of God" (28:23). The adverse response to Paul's message in Jerusalem (described in Acts 21:17—24:27) leads to his arrest. He is then sent to Caesarea to thwart an alleged plan of some Jewish leaders to kill him.

• Take a look at the events leading up to the trial and Paul's defense before Felix in Acts 24. Start by reading Acts 21:17-36. Make a list of the sequence of events and what triggers them. Why is Paul arrested by Roman soldiers when it is the Jewish crowd that is upset with him?

• Read Acts 21:37—22:30 and identify the main points of Paul's defense before his Jewish compatriots. Paul's speech includes an account of his encounter with the risen Christ on the way to Damascus. How does this address concerns the Jews in Jerusalem may have had about Paul? How does the crowd respond to him?

• Finally, read Acts 23 and list what Paul says and what happens to him as a result. Why is Paul sent to Felix, the governor of Caesarea?

3. As we have seen in previous sessions, there are many parallels between Acts and the Gospel of Luke. The Gospel tells the story of Jesus, which continues through his followers in Acts. There are notable similarities between the report of Paul's trial before Roman authorities in this section of Acts and Luke's account of Jesus' trial before Pilate. Jesus and Paul do not violate any Roman laws per se, yet both are tried and executed by Roman authorities.

• Read Luke 23:1-25. Underline or highlight the parallels between the trials of Jesus and Paul. What are the charges against Jesus and Paul, from a Roman perspective? What is the role of the crowd or mob in these trials? Compare and contrast how Jesus and Paul defend themselves.

• Discuss how Jesus and Paul are innocent in the sense that they have not violated Roman law, but both are condemned by Roman authorities. What are the Romans most concerned with in these cases? Why are Jesus and Paul perceived as threats? In what ways do the Jewish and Roman authorities cooperate with one another, and how do both benefit from this?

4. In Acts "the Way" is depicted as a movement within Judaism. In Paul's perspective the beliefs and practices of these early followers

Notes

of Jesus are in line with Jewish law and the prophets. And yet in the closing chapters of Acts, Paul's antagonists are Jews. Why is this?

• The Gospel of Luke and Acts link Jesus' resurrection with the mission to the Gentiles (see Luke 24:44-47 and Acts 26:22-23), and this inclusion of Gentiles seems to be a sticking point with other Jews. Why might other Jews be concerned about the mission to the Gentiles? What are your reactions to this issue?

5. Paul's letters to the Philippians and Philemon were written from prison. In the session Scripture text and elsewhere in Acts, Paul is also portrayed as a prisoner. Like Jesus, he maintains his innocence but is nonetheless regarded as suspect by Roman authorities. The trials and executions of Jesus and Paul raise questions about the activity of Jesus and his followers in relation to the state and its judicial system.

• Crucified as an enemy of the Roman order, Jesus was raised from the dead. What does this say about power? What does it say about the political significance of the resurrection for Jesus' followers then and now?

• Read Acts 24:5 again and note the charges brought by Tertullus, spokesman for the high priest, to the governor Felix. In the end, Jesus and Paul are both arrested and tried before Roman judicial authorities for stirring up the people or disturbing the status quo. What does this tell us about the Jesus movement and society? Do we expect the Spirit acting through us to disrupt the status quo? Why or why not? What might that look like in our day?

Historical Context

1. The *Pax Romana* began in 27 B.C.E. (the Latin word *pax*, most often translated "peace," also means "treaty" or "accord"). This peace meant the absence of war within the empire and the rule of law, both of which were enforced when needed. Roman legions patrolled the borders with success, and though there were still many foreign wars, territory belonging to the empire was free from invasion, piracy, or social disorder on any grand scale.

• Read Acts 24:2 and note how Tertullus refers to Felix and the "peace" in the Roman Empire. The Roman historian Tacitus, writing around the same time as Luke, describes Felix as a governor who "practiced every kind of cruelty and lust, wielding the power of a king." Moreover, rather than promoting peace, Tacitus also reports that Felix increased the problems in Judea. With this information, what do you think about the introductory statement made by Tertullus?

• Though Paul and other followers of Jesus do not directly criticize the Roman Empire, in Acts we see the contrast between Roman politics and justice and the values and practices of Paul and the "sect of the Nazarenes." List some of the tensions and potential conflicts you see between Rome and "the Way." What tensions and potential conflicts do you see between church and state today? When might faithfulness to the gospel today lead to legal or political tensions or civil disobedience?

• In Acts the church is a faithful presence in the world, bearing witness to the kingdom of God in public but not entwined with the political system except to defend itself. In today's world, what are some ways the church can be a public witness to the good news of God's kingdom without getting entangled in the politics of the state?

2. The issue of power is another important aspect of the political context of Acts in general and Paul's trial before Felix specifically. Paul and the majority of Jesus' followers have marginal social status and few privileges compared to the aristocratic elites before whom they must give a defense. In the trial scenes of both Paul and Jesus, the power brokers of both the Jewish and Roman political systems interrogate a Jew who has no worldly power or status to speak of and yet bears witness to the one who created the world and has the power to bring life out of death.

• How is the world's idea and experience of power different from God's power? How have you experienced the power of the resurrection in your own life or observed it at work in the world?

• Power is part and parcel of the human experience, says James Hunter Davidson (*To Change the World: The Irony, Tragedy and Possibility of Christianity in the Late Modern World*, Oxford, 2010). It is not a matter of being powerful or powerless, but rather of how we use the power we have and how we relate to those who have power in the world. How does Paul in Acts 24 use the power he has? How does he engage those who have power in the world? How will the church and its people use the power we have? How will the church engage the world?

Lutheran Context

1. Righteousness and justification are key concepts in Lutheran theology. The Greek word for "justice" is also translated as "righteousness" in the New Testament and is related to "justification" language. In the Bible these terms have to do with being in "right relationship" with God and other human beings. In a Roman context, justice and righteousness involved the *Pax Romana* and the preservation of order at all costs, through force and rule of the law.

• Reread Acts 24:24-25. How would you describe this encounter between Paul, Felix, and Drusilla? List some reasons Felix might have become afraid.

 Notes

Notes

• A distinction is sometimes made between justice based on punishment or payback and justice aimed at restoring what has been lost. What kind of justice do you see in the trial of Paul before Felix? What kind of justice is characteristic of God? Give some examples of how you see God's justice at work in the world. What is the relationship between God's justice and God's mercy?

Devotional Context

1. In Acts Jesus' resurrection is not so much a doctrine or belief as it is an experience of the risen Jesus through the Spirit's power. When the risen Jesus appears to his followers in the Gospels, he commissions them to share the good news with others. The mission of the early church in Acts hinges entirely on the resurrection of Jesus, which shows the transforming power of God's love to bring about the new creation.

• How do you bear witness to the resurrection in your daily life?

• Martin Luther connects our experience of Jesus' resurrection to baptism. Read his explanation of baptism in *Luther's Small Catechism with Evangelical Lutheran Worship Texts* (Augsburg Fortress, 2008, pp. 28–30) or in ELW (pp. 1164–1165). Contemplate how "a new person is to come forth and rise up to live before God in righteousness." How have you experienced dying with Christ—that is, what in you and around you is dying that something new might be born? How have you experienced being raised with Christ?

Wrap-up

Be ready to look back over the work your group has done in this session.

Pray

Life-giving God, in the mystery of Christ's resurrection you send light to conquer darkness, water to give new life, and the bread of life to nourish your people. Send us forth as witnesses to your Son's resurrection, that we may show your glory to all the world, through Jesus Christ, our risen Lord. Amen. (Easter Prayer, ELW p. 65)

Extending the Conversation

Homework

1. Read the next session's Bible text: Acts 28:1-31.

2. Brainstorm a list of various forms and expressions of power. How does power work in the world? How do you see God's power at work in the world? How would you characterize God's power?

Enrichment

1. If you wish to read through the entire book of Acts during this unit, read the following sections this week:

Day 1: Acts 25:1-27
Day 2: Acts 26:1-18
Day 3: Acts 26:19-32
Day 4: Acts 27:1-12
Day 5: Acts 27:13-25
Day 6: Acts 27:26-44
Day 7: Acts 28:1-31

2. Throughout the week pay attention to the pattern of dying and rising in the world, in nature, in your community, and in your own life. Write or journal about how trust in a God who brings life out of death affects the way you look at death and life.

For Further Reading

Notes on Acts 24:1-27 in *Lutheran Study Bible*, *The HarperCollins Study Bible*, or *The New Oxford Annotated Bible*.

The Acts of the Apostles, by Luke Timothy Johnson, pp. 409–425.

Notes

Acts 28:1-31

Learner Session Guide

Focus Statement

In his trial before Felix, Paul claimed he had done nothing against Jewish or Roman law, and appealed his case to Caesar. Acts ends with Paul under house arrest in Rome, where he continues to witness to the kingdom of God.

Key Verse

He lived there two whole years at his own expense and welcomed all who came to him, proclaiming the kingdom of God and teaching about the Lord Jesus Christ with all boldness and without hindrance. Acts 28:30-31

And So We Came to Rome

Focus Image

The Apostle Paul, c. 1657, Rembrandt van Rjin, Widener Collection, Courtesy National Gallery of Art, Washington.

Gather

Check-in

Take this time to connect or reconnect with the others in your group and give a special welcome to newcomers. The final chapter of Acts narrates Paul's journey to and arrival in Rome, where Luke's version of the story of the early church concludes with Paul under house arrest for two years. This story begins on the island of Malta after the ship carrying Paul to Rome runs aground. On Malta Paul receives hospitality from the islanders. From there he goes to Rome, where he meets local Jewish leaders and fellow believers. Although Paul has been a key figure in the expansion of "the Way" westward throughout the Roman Empire, most Jews have not embraced the gospel about Jesus. Nonetheless, Paul emphasizes one last time to Jewish leaders in Rome that "it is for the sake of the hope of Israel that I am bound with this chain" (Acts 28:20).

Pray

Lord, you are the giver of all life. We surrender to you the seemingly dead things, the hopeless-looking things of our lives. We offer you the deep places in our hearts, the places that feel cut off, dried up, the places where all hope is lost. Come, Holy Spirit, and breathe on the barren places of our hearts that we may know you are the Lord. Amen.

Focus Activity

The Focus Image is Rembrandt's portrait of the apostle Paul. Paul has been the chief character in the second half of Acts, which has shown him as a prophet and a proclaimer of the dawn of God's kingdom through the death and resurrection of Jesus. Rembrandt's rendering depicts an older Paul in contemplation, surrounded by the tools of his trade, prepared to write a letter. (You may have noticed that Acts does not mention Paul's letters.) How did you picture Paul when you started this study of Acts? How do you see him now? Imagine that Rembrandt's portrait is of Paul under house arrest in Rome. What is Paul thinking? What concerns does he have?

Open Scripture

Read Acts 28:1-31.

- As you listen to the passage with your heart, what words or phrases speak to you?

- What surprises you?

- What questions do you have?

Join the Conversation

Literary Context

1. The theme of salvation for all people begins in Luke 1–2 and continues through the end of Acts. Reread Acts 28 and note how Paul affirms the fulfillment of God's promises for both Jews and Gentiles.

- Read Acts 13:46-47 and 18:5-6 along with 28:28. What circumstances or conditions cause Paul to turn to the Gentiles? What are the ramifications of this for Jews? How are Paul's mission to the Gentiles and God's promises to Israel related?

Notes

Notes

• Just as the Gospel of Luke depicts Jesus as a prophet who proclaims and enacts the kingdom of God, Acts presents Paul as a prophetic figure whose proclamation of the kingdom is accompanied by signs. Read Luke 17:20-21. As you reflect on your study of Acts, discuss some ways that Jesus' statement "The kingdom of God is among you" (Luke 17:21) rings true in Acts.

• Paul continues to proclaim the kingdom of God in Rome, which was a kingdom of sorts itself, where the emperor was regarded as sovereign over the land and the people. Is there any indication in Acts 28 or elsewhere in Acts that Rome regards Paul's message about God's kingdom as subversive or a challenge to imperial authority? Why or why not?

2. Throughout Luke–Acts hospitality is an important symbol of receptivity to God. Welcoming Jesus' followers is tantamount to opening one's heart to God, and, conversely, Jesus' followers convey God's grace to strangers. Hospitality is also linked to the sharing of possessions.

• Locate the island of Malta on the map on page 61. Reread Acts 28:1-10 and note how hospitality is shown here.

• Read Luke 10:1-12, which describes Jesus sending out seventy-two followers and impressing upon them the importance of hospitality in their mission. How does this passage shed light on the encounter between Paul and the people of Malta? What is the role of kindness and hospitality in sharing the gospel of Jesus with others in Acts, and in the world today?

• Paul interacts with Gentiles and Jews in Acts 28. Discuss how the gospel shapes our relationships with those who do not share faith in Christ, and what the church can learn from Acts 28 about how to engage others in mission.

3. Since the controversy caused by his visit to Jerusalem (Acts 21), Paul has been brought before the Roman judicial system, first in Caesarea and now in the capital city of Rome. However, the Roman authorities in Caesarea and Rome do not appear to be very concerned about Paul. Moreover, the Jews in Rome do not even attempt to make a case against Paul. Rather, after Paul arrives in Rome, the writer of Acts seems more interested in clarifying the relationship between Paul's gospel and mission on the one hand and Judaism on the other.

• Read Acts 1:6-8 and 28:17-20. Talk about Paul's hopes for Israel in Acts 28, and how the Jews respond to his message.

• Isaiah 6:9 is quoted in Acts 28:26-27 and in Jesus' parable of the sower in Luke 8:1-10. Look at these three passages. What is being said in Luke and Acts about the Jews' lack of response to the message of God's kingdom? What significance does this have for mission today?

 Notes

4. Endings are important in letters, books, plays, and movies because they present important ideas and issues that tend to linger in the hearts and minds of an audience. In Acts 28 Paul arrives in Rome to stand trial, but a trial never takes place. We know, however, that Paul was eventually executed in Rome. Luke wrote Acts at least twenty years after this, but chose not to mention Paul's death, even though he probably knew about it.

• How did you expect Luke's account of Paul's mission and the expansion of the early Christian movement to end? Discuss your reactions to the ending and the main ideas it conveys.

• The writer could have brought some closure to this narrative of the Way, but instead he provides a rather open-ended conclusion to the story. Use your imagination and what you have learned from your study of Acts to elaborate on how the story continues. What happens during the two years that Paul is under house arrest in Rome? Does the gospel spread in Rome? What kind of obstacles do Paul and his coworkers face as they continue to teach about the kingdom of God?

Historical Context

1. When Paul arrives in Rome he is greeted by fellow believers (Acts 28:14-15). The first Christ followers in Rome came from Jerusalem shortly after the death and resurrection of Jesus in the 30s c.e. There was a significant Jewish population in Rome, and the communities of Christ there were house churches closely affiliated with the synagogues. The Roman historian Seutonius reports that in 49 the emperor Claudius "expelled from Rome the Jews constantly making disturbances at the instigation of Chrestus." Acts 18:1-2 and 18:18-19 report that Priscilla (sometimes called Prisca) and Aquila went to Corinth when Jews were sent out of Rome, and later accompanied Paul to Ephesus, where he left them and departed for Jerusalem. In 54 Nero succeeded Claudius as emperor and allowed Jews to return to Rome. Paul wrote his letter to Roman believers sometime in the period 56–57, when Jewish believers in Christ had returned to Rome and to what had become a predominantly Gentile movement in their absence. Paul probably arrived in Rome sometime in 60. He was executed in 62.

• In Paul's letter to the Romans it appears that the Gentile majority was discriminating against the Jewish minority and claiming to displace it (see Romans 14:1; 11:17-24). In what ways might Paul's message to Jews in Acts 28:17-31 be a response to anti-Judaism in Rome and in Roman communities of Christ?

• Talk about what we can learn from Paul about interpreting and communicating the revelation of God through Jesus in ways that

Notes

are sensitive to and respectful of Jews and people of other faiths, without compromising our faith in Christ.

- By the time Luke writes Acts, the Way is still a movement within Judaism, but Gentiles have been more responsive to the gospel and make up the majority of believers. God's faithfulness and impartiality are important themes in Paul's letter to the Romans. Although not as explicitly developed in Acts, these same convictions seem to undergird the writer's perspective. Luke tells the story of Jesus and his followers as a story about the restoration of Israel, and yet Gentiles embrace the gospel more than Jews. How do we understand and tell the story of Jesus and the early church in a way that emphasizes God's faithfulness and impartiality beyond our own faith tradition?

2. Although Paul goes to Rome to appeal charges made against him by Jews in Jerusalem, he does not do this once he is in Rome. And on their side, the Jews in Rome do not seem interested in supporting the charges against Paul made by the Jewish authorities in Jerusalem. It's possible that they didn't receive information about the charges against Paul. Perhaps they lacked the motivation to pursue those charges. The Roman judicial system was weighted in favor of those of high status who could afford an advocate, and Jews in Rome had lower social and economic status.

- Reread Acts 28:21-22. Why might the followers of Jesus have had a negative reputation among Jews? What is the reputation or perception of Christians among those outside the church today? What positive and negative things do people have to say about the role of the church in society? How should the church respond to these criticisms?

3. Why is Paul still held as a prisoner when there appears to be no case against him? Acts doesn't give a reason. It simply reports that Paul is under house arrest in Rome for two years while he continues to preach and teach. According to tradition Paul was later executed in Rome. The church historian Eusebius writes that Paul was beheaded in Rome during Nero's rule and that Peter was likewise crucified (*Eccl. Hist.* 2.25.5).

Neither Jesus nor Paul is guilty of breaking any Jewish or Roman laws, yet both are tried and executed. The only reason the Romans executed people was for sedition, that is, for subversive behavior that disrupted the imperial order. Although Luke does not directly challenge the Roman judicial system, the innocence of Jesus and Paul in Luke–Acts is at least a tacit indictment of imperial justice.

- Why doesn't the writer Luke pose a more direct challenge to the Roman order? Is Luke defending the early Christian movement

Notes

to the Roman Empire by trying to show that it is not a subversive movement or a threat to imperial order or justice? Is the Way a subversive movement? Why or why not? Discuss the contrast in Acts between the depiction of God's justice and imperial justice.

Lutheran Context

1. Lutherans and other Christians often talk about the life of faith as a journey. The central section of the Gospel of Luke (Luke 9:51—19:27) is known as the travel narrative because Jesus teaches his followers about the reality and practices of the kingdom of God on the way to Jerusalem. In Acts the movement of Jesus' followers is called "the Way" and the story of Paul's mission and imprisonment is depicted as a journey. In a sense the entire biblical narrative, from Genesis to Revelation, can be described as a journey to and from God. The one constant in the story is God's faithfulness, which is emphasized throughout Acts.

• As you reflect on your own journey in light of your study of Acts, what are you learning about who you are and your relationship with God? What have you discovered about God's faithfulness? What have you learned about the church?

2. Lutheran pastor Dietrich Bonhoeffer was imprisoned in Nazi Germany and martyred in 1945 for his faith in Christ. In his prison cell he began a pilgrimage he never intended to take. Torn from family and friends and all he loved, he found that he didn't really know himself. His poem "Who Am I?" (published in *Letters and Papers from Prison*, Touchstone, 1997) concludes:

Who am I? They mock me, these lonely questions of mine.
Whoever I am, Thou knowest, O God, I am Thine!

• When life has been difficult for you, what have you learned about what it means to belong to God? Write about this.

Devotional Context

1. Followers of Jesus are involved in spiritual or faith practices throughout Acts. List some of these practices—the ways believers lived out their faith, anticipating and participating in the kingdom of God. If you wish, add other personal and communal spiritual practices to your list. How do spiritual practices connect you to God and to others?

2. Paul and his coworkers testified in word and deed to God's kingdom of love and justice. How will you testify to God's kingdom of love and justice? Name some ways your congregation and the church can enact God's love and justice in the world.

Notes

Wrap-up

Be ready to look back over the work your group has done in this session.

Pray

Father, hallowed be your name.
Your kingdom come.
Give us each day our daily bread.
And forgive us our sins,
for we ourselves forgive everyone indebted to us.
And do not bring us to the time of trial.
(Luke 11:2-4)

Extending the Conversation

Homework

1. Review journal entries or notes you have written during this study of Acts. How has the Spirit been at work in and through you?

2. Create a drawing, painting, sculpture, poem, song, or dance that expresses something you have learned about the Holy Spirit.

Enrichment

1. Consider reading or studying the Gospel of Luke as a group.

2. Do some research on Paul, Peter, and others who died because of their faith in the God who raised Jesus Christ from the dead. What effect has martyrdom had on the growth of Christianity?

For Further Reading

Notes on Acts 28:1-31 in *Lutheran Study Bible*, *The HarperCollins Study Bible*, or *The New Oxford Annotated Bible*.

The Acts of the Apostles, by Luke Timothy Johnson, pp. 460–476.

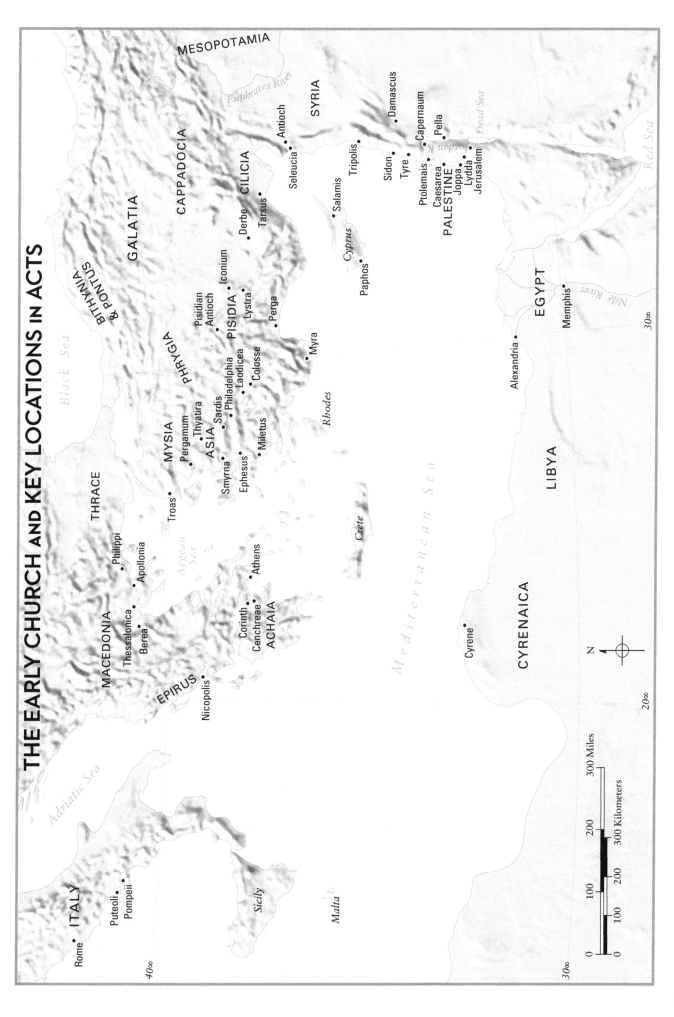

THE EARLY CHURCH AND KEY LOCATIONS IN ACTS

CPSIA information can be obtained
at www.ICGtesting.com
Printed in the USA
LVHW060313160422
715912LV00023B/78

9 781451 402742